POR EL
BIEN
COMÚN

POR QUÉ

EXISTEN REGLAS EN LA ESCUELA

PATRICK HELY

TRADUCIDO POR ESTHER SARFATTI

PowerKiDS press.

New York

Published in 2019 by The Rosen Publishing Group, Inc.
29 East 21st Street, New York, NY 10010

First Edition

Translator: Esther Sarfatti
Editorial Director, Spanish: Nathalie Beullens-Maoui
Editor, Spanish: Natzi Vilchis
Editor, English: Jennifer Lombardo
Book Design: Tanya Dellaccio

Photo Credits: Cover Sergey Novikov/Shutterstock.com; p. 5 wavebreakmedia/Shutterstock.com; p. 7 gpointstudio/ Shutterstock.com; p. 9 vgajic/E+/Getty Images; p. 11 RUSS ROHDE/Cultura/Getty Images; pp. 13, 19 Monkey Business Images/ Shutterstock.com; p. 15 Lorena Fernandez/Shutterstock.com; p. 17 kali9/E+/Getty Images; p. 21 Syda Productions/ Shutterstock.com; p. 22 ESB Professional/Shutterstock.com.

Cataloging-in-Publication Data

Names: Hely, Patrick.
Title: Por qué existen reglas en la escuela / Patrick Hely.
Description: New York : PowerKids Press, 2019. | Series: Por el bien común | Includes glossary and index.
Identifiers: LCCN ISBN 9781538335581 (pbk.) | ISBN 9781538335574 (library bound) | ISBN 9781538335598 (6 pack)
Subjects: LCSH: Schools–Juvenile literature. | Student etiquette–Juvenile literature.
Classification: LCC BJ1857.S75 H45 2019 | DDC 395.5–dc23

Manufactured in the United States of America

CPSIA Compliance Information: Batch #CS18PK: For Further Information contact Rosen Publishing, New York, New York at 1-800-237-9932

CONTENIDO

Tu comunidad escolar. 4

Venimos a aprender 8

Igualdad y seguridad 14

¿Quiénes hacen las reglas?. 18

Alcanza tus objetivos 22

Glosario 23

Índice. 24

Sitios de Internet. 24

Tu comunidad escolar

Una comunidad es un grupo de personas que viven o trabajan en el mismo lugar y se preocupan por las mismas cosas. A menudo, los miembros de la comunidad tienen valores e ideas similares. La gente puede pertenecer a varias comunidades, entre ellas su ciudad y su barrio. Tu escuela también es un tipo de comunidad.

Cuando la gente hace cosas que **benefician** a toda su comunidad, están trabajando por el bien común. Trabajar por el bien común ayuda a que una comunidad funcione mejor. También mantiene contentos a sus miembros. Una forma sencilla de contribuir, o dar algo, al bien común de tu comunidad escolar es seguir las reglas.

Venimos a aprender

Piensa en un día en tu escuela. Probablemente tengas que seguir muchas reglas. Es posible que incluso te parezca que son demasiadas reglas. Sin embargo, sin reglas habría caos o una falta total de orden. Las reglas son importantes porque ayudan a todo el mundo en tu comunidad escolar a **concentrarse** en aprender.

Cuando sigues las reglas, como quedarte en tu asiento, demuestras respeto por tus compañeros de clase que están tratando de aprender. Si te levantaras de tu asiento y te pusieras a correr, te convertirías en una distracción. Las distracciones son las cosas que alejan tu atención de lo que deberías hacer, como escuchar a tus maestros.

Las escuelas tienen reglas para que no haya problemas en los salones de clase o fuera de ellos. Cuando sigues las reglas, demuestras a tus maestros y a tus compañeros de clase que te importa tu **educación**. También demuestras que te importa la educación de tus compañeros. Esto mejora las **relaciones** entre alumnos y maestros, lo cual hace que tu escuela funcione mejor.

13

Igualdad y seguridad

Las escuelas tienen reglas para que todos los alumnos tengan la misma oportunidad de aprender. Seguramente en clase tienes que levantar la mano antes de hacer o contestar una pregunta. Esto es para que todo el mundo tenga la oportunidad de hablar. Las reglas que **prohíben** que copies las tareas o exámenes también sirven para proteger a los demás alumnos.

Gracias a las reglas, tu escuela es un lugar seguro para aprender, tanto dentro como fuera. Las reglas que prohíben correr por los pasillos ayudan a los alumnos a moverse por la escuela de manera segura. Muchos alumnos caminan o van en bicicleta a la escuela. Las reglas del estacionamiento y las que dicen cuándo y dónde puede manejar la gente su auto, también contribuyen a la seguridad de los alumnos.

¿Quiénes hacen las reglas?

Los directores y maestros crean las reglas de las escuelas. Trabajan por el bien de la comunidad escolar al hacer reglas que ellos consideran útiles, justas y buenas para todos. Cuando los alumnos siguen las reglas, demuestran que son **responsables** y confiables. Algunas veces, los alumnos tienen la oportunidad de ayudar a hacer las reglas de su escuela.

Si sigues las reglas, tus maestros y director se fijarán, y te lo **agradecerán**. También notarán si rompes una regla, y en ese caso podrías meterte en problemas. Por ejemplo, si gritas durante la clase, tal vez no te dejen salir durante el recreo. Si en tu escuela hay alguna regla que no comprendes, no tengas miedo de pedirle a un adulto que te la explique.

Alcanza tus objetivos

Las reglas ayudan a las comunidades escolares a ser seguras y permiten que sus alumnos se concentren en aprender. Al seguir las reglas demuestras respeto por tu educación y la de los demás. Las reglas en la escuela ayudan a los alumnos a alcanzar sus objetivos y a tener éxito.

GLOSARIO

agradecer: dar las gracias a alguien.

beneficiar: hacer algo bueno para alguien o algo.

concentrarse: poner mucha atención en una tarea.

educación: acción de aprender o enseñar.

prohibir: no permitir que se haga algo.

relación: conexión entre dos o más personas o cosas.

responsable: se refiere a la persona que hace lo correcto o hace las cosas que se esperan de ella.

23

ÍNDICE

A
alumnos, 12, 14,
    16, 18, 22
atención, 10

B
barrio, 4

C
caos, 8
ciudad, 4
comunidad, 4, 6, 8,
    18, 22

D
director/a, 18, 20
distracción, 10

E
educación, 12, 22

M
maestros, 10, 12,
    18, 20

O
objetivos, 22

P
preguntas, 14

R
recreo, 20
relaciones, 12
respeto, 10, 22

SITIOS DE INTERNET

Stay Safe, Play Safe

A Book About Safety Rules

By Barbara Seuling

Illustrated by Kathy Allert

Prepared with the cooperation of Bernice Berk, Ph.D., of the Bank Street College of Education

A GOLDEN BOOK • NEW YORK

Western Publishing Company, Inc.   Racine, Wisconsin 53404

Note to Parents

Teaching children to observe common safety rules in their day-to-day activities is a very important job. But it isn't enough just to tell children the rules—parents have to make sure the rules will be remembered and followed. Instructions such as "Don't do that," and "Stay away from this," are sometimes difficult for children to remember and follow. Children automatically turn off their listening apparatus if they hear a scolding tone of voice. That's why reading STAY SAFE, PLAY SAFE will help your child learn more easily. Presented in short, "what if…" vignettes, safety rules are given proper importance without being scary or intimidating. Children can enjoy hearing the story that sets up each situation, and can probably guess what the safety rule at the end will be.

STAY SAFE, PLAY SAFE should be reread often. On the second or third reading you might ask your child to tell you the safety rule, rather than reading it aloud. Making a game of reading the book can help reinforce your child's learning experience.

Most children will enjoy reminding everyone to follow the basic safety rules they've learned—and parents will enjoy seeing how much their children remember!

—The Editors

Everybody has jobs to do. Some people have jobs in stores, some in schools, and some in offices.

At home there are jobs, too. Someone gets the food ready for dinner, and someone makes sure the doors are locked at night.

There's one especially important job that is just right for you. That job is to help your family and friends stay safe, and play safe.

Suppose your dad says, "Let's go on a picnic!" Everyone gets everything they can think of: they fill the cooler chest with fried chicken, and sandwiches, and fruit punch, and potato chips, and pickles. They pack the car with the food, the dog, the fishing rod, the ball and catcher's mitt, the bathing suits, the maps, a flashlight, and the suntan lotion. Everyone gets in and you're ready to go.

But wait! Did you all remember to buckle your seat belts? If there's an accident, the seat belts can save lives.

It can be your job to make sure no one ever forgets to buckle his or her seat belt. You can say:

"BUCKLE UP!"

Suppose it's a sunny day, and you and your friend go to the park to play ball. While you're playing, your friend hits the ball way over the fence and the ball rolls across the street. The light is red and people are waiting on the curb for it to change. But your friend is in a hurry to get the ball so he can get back to the game.

He should be patient and wait until the light changes from red to green. But what if he doesn't? What if he runs into the street to go after the ball? He could get hurt.

Your job can be to remind your friend that he can always get a new ball, but you can't always find a good new friend. You can say:

"WAIT FOR THE GREEN!"

Suppose your cousin invites you to go sailing. You wear
a nylon windbreaker to keep you dry. You put on sneakers
or boat shoes with rubber bottoms so you won't slip. You
take a hat to keep the sun off your head. There is a
compass, and an emergency SOS siren in case you get lost,
or into trouble.

It looks as if your cousin has thought of everything, but something's missing. You aren't wearing your life jackets! If someone falls overboard, he can bob up and down like a cork until someone rescues him—but only if he's wearing a life jacket.

Your job can be to make sure each person on board is wearing one. You can say:

"WEAR YOUR LIFE JACKET!"

Suppose you're watching your little sister and she wants
to play cooking at the real stove. She wants to light a real
match.

You know you're not supposed to light the oven without
a grownup around.

Put the matches way up high out of her reach, and tell
her you'll play cowboys with her instead.

You can say:

"NEVER PLAY WITH FIRE!"

If you are *in* a fire, do you know how to get out safely?

Touch the door to see if it's hot. If it is, stay put. The fire is outside, so you're in the safest place.

If the door is cool, open it and go outside as quickly as you can.

If there's smoke, get down on your hands and knees where there's less smoke, and crawl out.

Then run for help, to a neighbor's house or to the fire alarm box.

Suppose you are riding your bike in the street, and another kid comes along on his bike and wants to tell you a joke. The kid starts clowning and showing off how he can ride with only one hand. Tricks are best in the backyard, not on the road. It would be better to talk and laugh later, when you're walking.

It can be your job to tell your friend these rules. You can say:

"STAY ON THE RIGHT!"

"RIDE SINGLE FILE!"

"RIDE WITH THE TRAFFIC!"

"KEEP BOTH HANDS ON THE HANDLEBARS!"

Suppose your aunt takes you and your cousin to the beach, and suddenly there's a big thunderstorm. Your cousin says, "Let's stay here under the umbrella to keep dry."

But that's the wrong thing to do. Lightning looks for tall things like trees, and poles—and beach umbrellas. As a matter of fact, even if you're short, *you* might be the tallest thing around.

People should fold up their umbrellas, gather up their belongings, and leave the beach quickly. Your job can then be to tell the others still stretched on the sand,

"GET OFF THE BEACH

DURING A THUNDERSTORM!"

Suppose you're visiting Grandma and Grandpa in the country, and Grandpa is going to take you for a walk at night to look at the stars. You're wearing a white shirt, but Grandma says, "Wear a jacket. There's a chill in the air."

It's dark out there, and your only jacket is dark blue. Drivers on the road can't see dark colors at night. You've got a job to do. Ask Grandpa if he has a light-colored jacket you can borrow, so drivers on the road can see you from a distance.

Grandpa is probably so pleased with how smart you are
that he gives you his favorite yellow sweater to wear. Then
he puts on a light blue jacket himself, and says just what
you're thinking:

"WEAR LIGHT COLORS AT NIGHT!"

Suppose you're home alone and there's a knock at the door. The person outside yells that his car broke down and all he wants to do is use your telephone. You shouldn't open the door for anybody. Only your mom or dad, with their own keys, can come in. What should you say?

Well...don't say anything. The person will probably think no one is home, and go away. Remember:

NEVER OPEN THE DOOR FOR STRANGERS!

If the person stays around, call the operator, or—if you
know the number—the police. Tell them you need help.
You should know these three things when you call:

Your name_____

Your address _____

Your telephone number _____

Fill in the spaces now, with your parent's help. That
way you will have it handy if you need it.

Suppose you're in the playground with the little boy
next door. He follows you around copying everything you
do. You have a job to do. You can teach him how to stay
safe in a playground.

When you go over to the swings, tell him:

"DON'T STAND IN FRONT OF THE SWINGS!"

When you go on the seesaw, the little boy wants to seesaw, too. Tell him:

"DON'T BOUNCE AROUND ON THE SEESAW!"

You go to the monkey bars and climb to the very top. The little boy climbs up after you. He gets scared, and starts to cry. Your job can be to show him how to get down—showing him where to put his hands and feet, and when to jump. Tell him:

"DON'T CLIMB HIGHER THAN YOU CAN HANDLE!"

Suppose you're watching TV with the whole family, and your little brother toddles out to the kitchen. He starts messing around with the things under the sink. Some of them could be dangerous. You have a job to do. Tell him:

"DON'T PLAY WITH ANYTHING UNDER THE SINK!"

Your job is to keep track of your little brother. Take any object away from him before he puts it in his mouth. You can say:

"DON'T PUT ANYTHING IN YOUR MOUTH!"

Lots of things look and smell good to a little child. A little child might think pills or medicines look like candy. They shouldn't be left within reach.

All medicines should have child-proof caps to protect small children who can't read labels. Older children have to be just as careful and not take any medicines, or anything to eat or drink that isn't clearly labeled.

DON'T TAKE PILLS OR MEDICINES UNLESS YOUR PARENTS GIVE THEM TO YOU!

Suppose your older cousin is visiting, and just before bedtime, she wants to take a bath. She gets her bathrobe, her slippers, a magazine, her French cologne, her bath salts, her huge Turkish towel, her perfumed soap, and her waterproof watch. On top of the pile in her arms is a radio.

She's got something dangerous in that pile. She shouldn't take the radio in with her or plug it in near the bath. Water and electricity should stay far apart.

Your job can be to tell your cousin that if she needs music, she can sing. You can say:

"DON'T PLUG ANYTHING IN WHEN YOU'RE WET!"

Now that you know all these safety rules, don't be surprised from now on, if everyone comes to you for advice!